Ali and Annie's Guide to...

Feeling Good about Yourself

Jilly Hunt

raintree

a Capstone company — publishers for children

Raintree is an imprint of Capstone Global Library Limited, a company incorporated in England and Wales having its registered office at 264 Banbury Road, Oxford, OX2 7DY – Registered company number: 6695582

www.raintree.co.uk
myorders@raintree.co.uk

Edited by Clare Lewis and Helen Cox Cannons
Designed by Dynamo
Original illustrations © Capstone Global Library Limited 2019
Picture research by Dynamo
Production by Tori Abraham
Originated by Capstone Global Library Limited
Printed and bound in India

ISBN 978 1 4747 7305 8
22 21 20 19
10 9 8 7 6 5 4 3 2 1

British Library Cataloguing in Publication Data
A full catalogue record for this book is available from the British Library.

Acknowledgements
We would like to thank the following for permission to reproduce photographs:
Getty Images: E+/ArtMarie, 17 Bottom Right, E+/kali9, 5 Top Right, E+/PeopleImages, 7 Bottom Right, E+/Sneksy, 4-5, E+/SolStock, 6-7, E+/Steve Debenport, 19, iStock/alla_iatsun, 22, iStock/alvarez, 14-15, iStock/DIGIcal, 9, iStock/Elenathewise, 15, iStock/embolk, 13, iStock/FatCamera, Cover, 1, 8, 24-25, iStock/Highwaystarz Photography, 23, iStock/kali9, 27, 28, iStock/KatarzynaBialasiewicz, 11, iStock/ljubaphoto, 21, iStock/Milkos, 16-17, iStock/pixelheadphoto, 20; Shutterstock: Creative Travel Projects, 26, RimDream, 18.

We would like to thank Charlotte Mitchell for her invaluable help with the preparation of this book.

Every effort has been made to contact copyright holders of material reproduced in this book. Any omissions will be rectified in subsequent printings if notice is given to the publisher.

All the internet addresses (URLs) given in this book were valid at the time of going to press. However, due to the dynamic nature of the internet, some addresses may have changed, or sites may have changed or ceased to exist since publication. While the author and publisher regret any inconvenience this may cause readers, no responsibility for any such changes can be accepted by either the author or the publisher.

Contents

I'm Ali! Look out for our helpful tips throughout the book.

Hi! I'm Annie and this is my dog, Charlie.

Some words are shown in bold, **like this**. You can find out what they mean by looking in the glossary.

Feeling good

Feeling good about yourself can make you happier. There are lots of ways you can do this. The choices you make can help you have a healthy mind and a healthy body.

▲ Spending time with good friends can help us to feel good.

Playing with a pet is a good way to have fun and forget any worries.

You can also help other people feel better about themselves. Being kind to your friends and family makes them feel good. It can make you feel good too.

Look after your body

Your body needs certain things to work well. It needs sleep and exercise. And it needs the right kinds of food and drink. Eating plenty of fruit and vegetables is a great way to look after your body.

TIP

You should aim to drink six to eight glasses of water a day.

Eating healthy food gives your body the energy you need to grow and be **active**.

Your body also needs water to work properly. Be careful about the other drinks you choose. Many drinks are very sugary. They are bad for your body and teeth. So are too many sweet snacks.

▲ Milk contains lots of the **vitamins** and **minerals** that our bodies need to stay healthy.

Get active

When you exercise, your body releases **hormones** that make you feel good. Exercise helps you to stay fit. It strengthens your muscles and bones. Being active even helps you to sleep better.

▲ We should aim for at least 60 minutes of exercise every day.

Being active with friends helps you to build your **confidence** and social skills. Social skills are things like being able to talk with other people and play together. Perhaps you could join a sports team or go to the park with your friends.

Did you know exercise is good for your mind? Exercise helps to improve your memory.

▲ Being active is fun!

Go to sleep!

You feel good after a full night's sleep. If you don't get enough sleep, you can feel grumpy. You might also find that it's harder to concentrate on your work at school.

▶ This chart shows the amount of sleep that you should get at different ages. But this is just a guide – not everybody needs the same amount of sleep.

Age		Hours of sleep needed
Newborn 0-3 months		14-17
Infant 4-11 months		12-15
Toddler 1-2 years		11-14
Preschool 3-5 years		10-13
School Age 6-13 years		9-11
Teenager 14-17 years		8-10
Young Adult 18-25 years		7-9
Adult 26-64 years		7-9
Older Adult 65 years		7-8

▲ Reading books is a great way to get ready for a good night's sleep.

While you sleep your body is busy. Your body uses this time to heal itself. Your brain is dealing with the new things you have seen or heard that day. Your **short-term memory** goes into your **long-term memory**. This helps you to learn things.

TIP

Try not to look at a digital screen, such as an iPad or TV, for at least an hour before bedtime. Screens keep your mind active. Then it can be hard for you to calm down and get to sleep.

Look after your mind

Being active helps your body but also helps your mind. You can make your mind feel good in other ways too. The way you think about a situation can make a difference.

Imagine you are learning a new skill, like climbing. Do you look at the highest climbing frame and think, "I'll never do that!"? Or do you look at a lower climbing frame and think, "I can do that!"?

Try setting yourself small goals. It's easier to see your progress if you break a task up into smaller steps.

▶ What do you think when you see a big challenge in front of you?

Be kind to yourself

It's easy to be hard on yourself and focus on problems. But that won't make you feel good. Instead, think of all the things you can do. Believe in yourself and what you can do.

TIP

Make a list of all the things that you can do and look at it when you feel sad. Here's my Top 3:
1. I can click my fingers really loudly.
2. I am kind.
3. I can make people laugh.

Keep trying at the things that you are still learning to do. You will do it!

▲ Focus on what you can do.

Make mistakes

Don't worry about making mistakes. We all make mistakes – it's how we learn. If you make a mistake it means you are learning.

If you don't understand something ask for help. Don't be scared about asking a question. You are still learning. You are probably not the only one who doesn't understand.

Making a mistake also means you are trying new things. If you are frightened of making mistakes you won't try new things.

TIP

I used to worry about making a mistake at school. But now I ask my teacher for some more help.

▲ You could be missing out on lots of fun if you don't ever try new things.

Learn to fail

When something isn't going to plan, don't give up. Perhaps you can't do a maths sum. Stop and think. Could you work it out if you did something different? What are you missing? It is important not to give up. This makes you **resilient**.

Nobody gets everything right first time.

▲ Keep trying and you will succeed.

Think of failure as not getting the result you want – yet. Think of it as a chance to grow. Tell yourself that you can learn to do anything you want. You might not be the best at something right away. But it's important to keep trying. Imagine how you will feel when you finally get there.

Share your worries

Sharing your worries can make you feel better. You could talk to a parent, teacher or friend. They will help you to work out how to solve your problems.

TIP

I talk to my mum when I'm worried about something. She helped me to work out what to do when I fell out with my friends.

Talking can make your problems seem smaller.

If you are upset you start breathing more quickly. Take some deep breaths. Count to six as you take a big breath. Then breathe out as you count to six again. Keep doing this until you start to feel calmer.

▲ Taking deep breaths helps you to feel calmer.

Think of others

Did you know you've got a special power? You can make others feel good about themselves just by being kind. When you are kind to others, your brain releases a **chemical**. This chemical makes you feel happier.

A kind word or action can make your friends or family happier.

Some people try to make themselves feel better by being unkind to other people. Perhaps they think it makes them look clever or strong. But can you really feel better about yourself if you've been mean?

TIP

Set yourself a goal to make someone smile today. How does it feel?

▲ We enjoy spending time with friends who are kind to us.

We're all different

Sometimes you might be tempted to compare yourself with others. Maybe you think your friends are better or happier than you. This might make you feel sad. You need to remember that we all have good days and bad days.

▶ If we were all the same, life would be boring.

Don't believe everything you see

It's also tempting to compare yourself with images you see in the **media**. You might see pictures of people in magazines, online or on TV. You might think that a person looks better than you. Or perhaps that they are happier than you.

It's good to remind yourself that these images aren't all real. Sometimes the photos have been altered with **filters** to make the person look a certain way. An actor might be wearing special make-up that makes them look good on camera.

▲ This is the photo without any filters.　▲ This is the photo using filters.

This is the photo before it was changed.

This is the photo after it was changed.

It's your choice

There are lots of choices you can make to feel good about yourself. Think about what you eat and drink. Be active. Be kind. Be brave and try new things – even if you might fail. Then feel proud of yourself when you finally achieve your goals. You can't do it all on your own, so talk to someone you trust if you're worried.

Ali and Annie's advice

* Think about when you did something for someone else that made you feel good.

* Make a list of all the things you can do.

* Keep adding new skills to your list.

* Set yourself small goals.

* Eat at least five portions of fruit and vegetables every day. A portion is the amount you can fit in the palm of your hand.

* Make healthy food choices and limit how many treats you have.

* Clean your teeth at least twice a day.

* Wash your hands before you eat to avoid germs that make you feel ill.

* Celebrate your achievements.

* Have fun!

Glossary

active to keep moving, like when you exercise or play. Your brain is active too, as it is always busy.

chemical basic substance

confidence belief in yourself and what you can do

filter digital tool that is used to change the way a photograph looks

hormones substances made by your body that act like messengers. Different hormones tell different parts of your body what to do.

long-term memory information you remember for a long time

media way of communicating, such as TV, magazines, newspapers or the internet

minerals natural substances that our bodies need to stay healthy

resilient keep trying and never give up

vitamins natural substances that our bodies need to stay healthy

short-term memory information you remember for only a short time

Find out more

Books

100 Things to Know About Food (Usborne, 2017)

How Are You Feeling Today? Molly Potter (Featherstone, 2014)

No Worries! Katie Abey (Studio Press, 2017)

Websites

www.nhs.uk/change4life

The Change4life website has lots of ideas to help you stay healthy.

www.childline.org.uk/info-advice/bullying-abuse-safety

If you want help about anything, from bullying to exams, visit the Childline website.

Index